To
Rosa Williams
With all good wishes
M Rahman



# Blush of the Rainbow

## A Selection of 100 Love Poems

Mojibur Rahman

PUBLISH AMERICA

PublishAmerica
Baltimore

First printing

ISBN: 1-4137-7552-7
PUBLISHED BY PUBLISHAMERICA, LLLP
www.publishamerica.com
Baltimore

Printed in the United States of America

I dedicate this book to all who touched my life like an awakening breeze. To ones without whom I could not possibly be complete.
Specially my family, who gave me inspiration and sense of belonging.
Above all my parents, my brothers and sisters who molded me to what I am today.

## Acknowledgments

My thanks go to Patricia Hardy for her painstaking effort in going through all of these poems and her comments. I am also grateful to Dorothy Winters for her suggestions and feedback. Generally I am very thankful to all the members of my Writers Circle for their valuable criticism.

## List of Contents

## *A Precious Moment*

I have stolen a precious moment

from the busy times of your life

to create my fate with your feats

and call your kismet as my own.

Why do you hide the love that I seek?

That I saw when I gazed in your eyes.

And why do all little things that I do?

Turn against the craze I have for you.

It is the deep pain of hiding it safe

in my heart, this notion of distrust.

Often I feel that I may lose you

in the maze of will over and above.

I look for you in the sunshine and rain

and yes! My heart cries for your love.

Fate has linked your name with mine

and my life and love is in your hands

## *Love is...? A Spark*

It began with a spark.

Which led to the creation

Of what we are.

And love came to be

like the birth of stars

after the big bang.

The rule of creation is

to create, it has to destroy.

So to fall in love we set ablaze

feelings in our hearts.

And begin a fusion of intrigue

to erupt in waves of passion.

As the love grows

.

it begins to rule our lives.

Some times we are lucky

just to be happy.

And some times we're struck

with the bad luck.

Love is the spark of creation.

Love is the seed of emotion.

Love is to gleam like stars.

Love is the key to what we are.

## *Blush of the Rainbow*

My love is the blush of the rainbow.

And he is mine to be an emotional show.

Like the rain tears pour from my eyes.

When the man I love meets her but denies.

He dispels the outpour of my love

and shines on the mist of her charm.

It needs my rain of care and his sunshine

to make a rainbow that he should know.

Soon he will find the mist has vanished.

and sunshine now reigns alone.

The rain has drifted to another land

for storm of hurt has lent a hand.

I am the rain and he is my sunshine.

If he wants me to shower upon him

and make our lives a nest of love.

He just has to make the rainbow blush.

## *All My Dreams*

Love letters that I write to you.
Aren't just to show my feelings.
They're my present and the future
and all my dreams I want to share.

Letters can't show my true feelings
and words can't mirror my desires.
But you can feel the poundings
of my heart with your heartbeats.

Every moment of my life that I breathe
is to make a chain of words for you.
While I think more loving words to write.
Just shout that you love my letters too.

## *Love is...? The Hands of Charm*

Head high! Like the trees of the forest.

Or stay low as a humble grass of the lawn.

I am either out of reach or trampled down

or made to behave like a clown.

There is no match for me to catch

when I do fall into the hands of charm.

Lost in this cruel forest of the people

trying to make friends of the kind.

Knowing not when and where to find

that special heart made of love.

They bring with them hidden hate.

Would I be able to find a right mate?

Lonely among the loners in need of love.

Left to bear ravages of the mortal beings.

Hot and tempered when it needs to be cool.

Drowning in kindness when there's no need.

At times it feels to be standing on the sky.

On my head, I often carry the Earth so high.

Love is to be calm when charm fails to catch.

Love is to be a loner when there isn't a match.

Love is to be selfish, humble and polite.

Love is for what all of us want to fight.

# *The Affair*

A man of steel toiling over the affair
he had with a woman he met in seminar.
He is really a softy at heart
made of wax not for everyone to know.
His wife invited a friend for a dinner
it was that woman he was shocked to find.

Ashamed to think that he had lied
to the woman for saying that one day,
he will marry her in earnest.
Though in his heart he didn't expect
to see her like this in his own house.
Now that she's here he risks losing his wife.

The inner wax of outer steel is to melt
by the heat of the hot plates of dinner.
And his only food for thought is meeting
her seated opposite at the dinning table.
He is ready to face the calamity
of the future as it unfolds before his wife.

The doorbell played the tune of Bolero
and his heart sank deeper with every tune.
His wife said, “It must be Jenny.
“Could you see to the door please?”
Door opened and his ring caught Jenny’s eye.
And she stood there with a smirk on her face.

## *Thank you*

I've thought

Quite a lot.

I have been

Very keen.

When inspired

I've admired.

I've kissed

When missed.

I have done

So often.

But not like this as such.

Thank you very much

## *Love is...? A Torrent of Bad Times*

A torrent of bad times

flows in the river of strife.

Along with the log of joy

and grains of good times.

I move on, fast or slow

on the highway of life.

At times with or without

the wishes of my heart.

What if grief sheds?

Tears from my eyes.

And I do not find

a friendly shoulder to cry.

Cast out and lonely

I keep on moving

and hope to find a friend

in times of my real need.

Then there are those

who have nowhere to go?

They look at the face

of life and wander alone.

This is the spell

I must cast to gain love.

Smile but do not shake

from the pain and heartache.

Love is a time of joy that flows in our veins.

Love is a smile playing on the lips of a child.

Love is a flood of pain drowning us in tears.

Love is what binds us together like a spell.

## *Love is...? A Fusion of Soul*

Like the hidden treasures of the ocean

from whence the microbial life began.

Like the restless tidal waves pounding

trying to reach the shores again and again.

Like, countless lonely hearts searching

for the basis of life and the reasons to live.

A truth rises to the surface from the deep

to feed love, the food of life from heaven.

Depth hides the view, as is the case.

Who is the first to unveil the face of desire?

Action of body, sight, scene and the vision

often leads to acquire the zeal of notion.

Tide of desire, and restless body and soul

draws near, the edges of unease to meet.

Strangers of the time to sail the boat of life

it really is the fusion of the moments in time.

Like allure of the ocean or charm of the hills
falling in love is neither a fall nor a rise.
It is the affairs of heart uplifting the soul
and cherished happiness of life ours to keep.
Like the tides, trying to reach the top of the hills
at times we do try to reach the depth of desire.
Revelations of the deep are rare but not so unique
but wonder of life, is not for living without love.

Love is the ocean of passion; all of us want to sail.
Love is the depth of feelings, restless to rise and fall.
Love is the waves of will, dashing at the edge of zeal.
Love is a fusion of soul with a chosen alien being.

## *The Mirror of Tomorrow*

I see in his eyes.

The mirror of tomorrow

The happiness is not

so easy to borrow.

Maybe at dawn

the tears of darkness

will spread the light.

In his starry eyes.

Then it will be me

in the mirror of tomorrow.

## The Last Time

Fell over a body that lay in a ditch

and I froze like a pack of ice.

The intensity at which

this tragedy has tormented

my whole being that a new

way of living has taken shape.

As I faced this strange incident

a sobbing call reached me

and a brush of cold breeze went past

urging me to see her for the last time

My feelings flared and in anxiety

as if I had stopped breathing.

But with the whisper in the air

my heart throbbed in sympathy

with the sound of footsteps

and I heard the cry again.

The smoky halo kept on calling.

Come on! I am here my love.

I glanced but there was no one

but a gush of breeze touching my face.

What was happening to me?

I did not know and shivered with fear.

I felt a touch on my shoulder

with the swish of the fresh air

and a rush of cold sweat bathed my spine.

But the glow of halo made me

to close my eyes and move

as if she was pulling me by the hand.

The figure went past the ditch

as if there was nothing there.

In the broken rhythm of a cry
she confessed to love me.
I stopped at the edge of the ditch
which the shrubs surrounded
filled with shallow murky water.
  She was calling and calling.
I moved ahead a few more steps
and fell over something cold and fleshy
lying half-submerged in the ditch.
And she held me for the last time.

## *Love is...? Your Thoughts*

Touch me with your thoughts

and hear love beats in your heart.

Try to get me out of your mind

and pain is all you will find

to live with in rest of your life.

Your thoughts always strike

me with the lightning of passion.

And I would like to come alive

in your dream once in a while.

You prefer to see through me

and rest your gaze on others.

While you are the one I worship

and my chants are your praise.

Love is a highway of thoughts.

Love is a one-track lane.

Love is a green signal of joy.

Love is a twin-engine plane.

# A Ball of Fire

Love is like a ball of fire

glowing with warmth and delight.

An answer to a heart's desire

a pleasure to cherish

or a torment to concede.

Like the world held by belief

or the force that binds us all.

Love is the heart of soul.

Love crushed by lust and greed.

Trapped by the soldiers of hate.

Is there no place to date?

Nowhere to hide our pride?

Sanity has seen better times.

But mystery of our hearts

of all ages, all nickels and dimes.

It's best without mimics or mimes.

If love is like a frozen place.

Pack ice carved like a face.

Where heart of life called love

does not have a place.

Then we'll have no option

but to change or keep in pace

with the other face of love called hate

and live our lives with regrets.

To live without love is vain

and to live with hate is foul.

But to be with love without care

is to live in heaven full of fear

## *Love is...? Clouds of Passion*

Rising clouds of passion cools
and pours like drizzle of care.
And chilled feelings begin to flow
like a stream of fear.
Then friendship takes a dive
in the pool of love.

Brushed by the breeze of kinship
I wish that my heart
shall rejoice the least.
The joy that may only last
till the end of the summer's day
even if my love isn't here to feast.

What grief will beat my heart?

When there're no beats to hear.

Black clouds of my feelings

have gone away to bear

the blessings that I have left

in some other land of love.

Love is just love, just right, no less no more.

Love is a blessing from God no less no more.

## *Embrace of Love*

Like the warm sunshine, I bathe
in his spell of glow and gaze.
He entices me to live with him
in an endless embrace of love.

Crazy it makes me, when I see him
dance cheek to cheek with other girls.
How to tell him about the hurt I feel
and the river of tears that I shed.

Let my curious eyes not to see

her, drawn to his spell of gaze.

While my cry for his concede

is not just a passing phase.

Here I stand in my resolve to win

his heart and soul by all means.

A day with him means more to me

than life not in his embrace of Love.

## *Somebody Else*

She made me find somebody else.

But when she is upset she runs to me.

Why does she use me the way she does?

I get hurt when she is out of my reach.

Would she be warm in the arms of others?

When I have given my whole life for her.

Maybe she is careless about her love.

I need to know if she didn't mean to be.

## *Words of Confession*

Summer is here to fade
clouds of my memory.
And let the rays
of the past days
focus at her and make
me peep through
the keyhole of my mind.
I see her smiling
just as she always did.
Those sweet confessions
together to live and die
is here to say goodbye.

Your promises take shape
in all colours and size.
Words of your confession
echo no sweet surprise.

The confession that you
love me still surrounds.
The places of confession
they are still around.
The park and the witness
tree shades, where we sat.
Whispering the words
Of confession in my ear.

How can I forget her confession?

The words are there to remind me.

The words of love found and lost.

The day we met the day we parted.

## *Love is...? Pain and Grief*

What am I without your love?

And what of this heart and mind.

I do know when my eyes meet yours

I feel immense pain and grief.

I need to share my smile and tears.

For me, are you there?

And when I cry for your love

from far or near it comes back to me.

With your love in my heart

all my dreams come alive.

And countless shades of joy

reasons with your cruel heart.

Love is the body.

Love is the soul

Love is the creation.

Love is all.

## *Like a Ring*

Am I just like a ring?

In your finger.

That you wear

to match your dress.

Why do you tease me?

Like a toffee to a child.

And serve to please me

to taste strong or mild.

I am not a wooden toy

that you carry in your car

I do have a beating heart

that's what I say so far.

You are mad about a change.

Like a girl about her curl.

So let me now change your ring

to match my heart's desire.

## *Marjie*

Marjie and I?

She with her dolls and I with my cars,

we played in the backyard

side by side with our own dreams.

We made our own ways.

I? I am a country singer.

and she? She's an art dealer.

The other day, she passed my way.

"Hey! she said. "I seem to know you, lad."

I went on singing like mad.

Would I go on singing?

Did she know the reason? I guess not.

Now that I'm a man and she's a woman.

Marjie! Let's play real mums and dads.

That won't be bad, real mums and dads.

Marjie and I!

## *I Believe*

I call witness that I believe.

Full moon is the face

I do know and admire.

Chill of the winter breeze

makes me aware and feel.

And how do I place you.

Do I take you as a friend

Or my love in disguise?

Should I smile and greet?

You are just a stranger!

Or have I gone made to believe

that you are a friend.

Do I bathe in your favour?

Yes! It is your kindness

or a cry for my heart's desire.

Surely not. It's not your love.

Come now pick your senses

and chain those charming words.

Lay aside the alliance of truth

to preach what is to be.

Sow the seeds of disgust

and let your wishes win.

Watch with your keen eyes.

What is false to be real.

How could it be?

That someone as you

holds the key

of friendship and well being.

And when I make a friend

or fall in love.

I am glad to believe

that my life is fulfilled

# A Falling Star

When I met you I was like a falling star.

Falling in love who knows why and where.

Now that you are mine but drifting apart.

Drifting in love who knows who to share.

When I kissed you my tired lips came alive.

Trembled with fear I knew but I didn't care.

And I was happy till the cold night did last.

Striving for love till the morning was there.

Regrets you left behind they do arise.

And I watch them they are always there.

Memories of you they'll always be mine.

To keep with me instead of love and care.

I won't break away like a falling star.

And don't forget that I am almost there.

Even though you left me hopeless so far.

My love I am here just for you to share.

## *Love is...? The Test to Bear*

Lips are to seal the secrets in our hearts
or broadcast a message for all to hear.
Either way, the gate is open or closed
and love or hate passes the test to bear.

Defiant lips cause an upset or hurt feelings
and when pleasing, sprays bliss all around.
When it tells a lie real than a truth.
The world stands at ease to listen.

At times it's better to shout aloud

and not play the routine of deaf and dumb.

Let the anger bubble up or love to vanish

in the mist of pride and insolence.

Love is a secret for us to keep.

Love is a bubble rising from deep.

Love is a pleasure to reach out for.

Love is a prize knocking at the door.

## *Show Your Feelings*

Love! Show your feelings

don't play a part.

Why are you changing?

The feel of your heart.

Why do you keep away?

When I try to come close.

Leave? There is no need.

You have nothing to heed.

Please wait for me
and take me with you.
Give me a chance?
To show I can change too.

The part I played in love
may have been poor.
So you changed your mind.
I was not quite aware.

## *Smile in Your Eyes*

I see love, smile in your eyes.

And tricks play on your lips.

It is in your nature to tease.

But what can I do, I love you.

Like a tune I hear, but can't see.

I know, you do not belong to me.

# *Dusk to Dawn*

You ask! How is my lonely soul?

What can I say? You know it all.

Sometimes it cries but carries on

searching for love from dusk to dawn.

How come you are here today?

Dried tears when you walked away.

Let the day go by while I cry.

Searching for love from dusk to dawn.

I am so sad I can't forget you.

Not long ago you loved me too.

So please come to me if you can.

I'll wait for you from dusk to dawn.

## *Love is...? Face of the Moon*

Like the changing face of the moon
our need for love changes over time.
Concern and care feeds its dawning
and sediment of wishes fills the end.

As a child passes through the age of youth
dreams turn into an action of a wise being,
From the age of concern to the middle age
we try to be happy in each and every event.

Like the hills and ridges of lunar landscape
love and hate fill the serene expanse of life.
And more often than not we are glad to find
that our love has grown on the fertile ground.

Love is the new moon in the span of life.
Love is the face we long to see in our dreams.
Love is the prize of care and legacy of youth.
Love is a ladder of life we climb in need.

## *Jealousy*

I burnt fiercely

in the fire of jealousy

by the thoughts of

me having a baby sister.

Being the only girl

I was the focus of love.

So I was happy

to wish for a brother.

Why did mum want

to have another girl?

It tormented me

all through day and night.

All kinds of worries

to hide inside me.

Would she be prettier?

And steal limelight.

Would she get all the love?

I used to despise.

Lived in worries though

she wasn't even born.

Months passed by

and I felt increasingly uneasy.

Just a little thought of her

made me crazy.

One day! At school

there was news on the phone.

I had a baby sister

and all my worries had gone.

The years quietly slipped away

masking our eyes.

And now I look at my

beautiful sister and I realise.

She is eight

and I'm fourteen years old.

She has everything I didn't

and she is so bold.

She's better than I could imagine.

As she grows older

and day by day I love her

even more as I behold her.

## *Love is...? A Blank Cheque*

I gave my soul like a blank cheque

for the worship of love.

She filled it with millions of wounds

and splinters of my belief

with her false promises and vows.

Do I still love her?

And like to forgive and forget.

I say no. This could only be

if she comes back to me

leaving all her past behind.

I will bear no pain of betrayal

and heal wounds of the past.

Love her to the extremes of desire

or the blank cheque would bounce back

to me from the end of eternity.

Love is to worship with body and soul.

Love is to forgive and forget it all.

Love is to smile at the face of adversity.

Love is to love till eternity.

## Love is...? The Girl Next Door

She is the girl next door
just beyond the edge of my wish.
Wall of her needs is not so clear
like the smile she wears.
Love sleeps deep in her heart
and joy plays with her fear.

There is a war of will inside me.
My heart is dying to be with her.
My mind says no to her company.
She is too vain to feel my love.

Watch her every day from afar

like the changing face of the moon.

How is it that she seems so cold?

Yet she heats my urge at every noon.

Love is the heartbeat that no one hears.

Love is the need that everyone bears.

## *Me!*

Me! With my splendor, pose and poise.

Colours of the rainbow hidden in my eyes.

Luring lips, glowing halo and blond hair

my one look and his pride float in the air.

By a blink of my eyes, I captivate the globe.

A lick of my lips narrows the widening slope.

With my long lashes, I plant love in his heart.

I'm well versed in love like an artist in his art.

Armed with beauty, poise glamour and gaze.

Fight the war of love setting his heart ablaze.

Then suddenly my joyous feeling turns sad.

Glued to the face of hurt I need love so bad.

Despite the rush of chaos at my life's tidal shore.

I gather my insight of love, beauty, and charms.

Put them to work like a solid plutonium core.

In the reactor of love, I am to melt in his arms.

## *Love is...? The Lyric*

I was the lyric of her love

and he was her chord.

She used me as her shield

and used him like a sword.

She played the chords without

the lyric when she felt sad.

And I did not know the reasons

of why she treated me so bad.

She knew no boundary at all.

Searched my heart like a lost soul.

Then she pretended not to know

my pain and felt no remorse.

Love is a lyric to sing with right chord.

Love is like a skylark needs to be free.

Love is like a nest for lovers to roost.

Love is a tune to play with a man like me.

# *Am* I?

Am I like the cold wind or a gush of fresh air?

From the stillness of the air

I steal the secret of peace

along with a wish and crave

to shower the thoughts of love.

Gently I touch the lives of many

or at time wake their feelings

just like the wind

or a gush of fresh air.

Am I like a gentle breeze or a violent storm?

When sleepy clouds of concern
cast a shadow upon my heart
and excite my whole being
like a gentle breeze.
Then with the rising tide of need
I fight the war of passion
to bring my wild desires to heed
just like a violent storm.

Am I not a friend or would be a soul mate?

Like a thunderstorm I tell the world
that my past was a midday dream.
Cheated by the chill of vow
but I was a friend indeed.
And the warm air of affection
blows through the hearts and minds
like a breeze, strong wind or violent storm
from the seed of friendship love has grown.

Yes! Love is in my heart and I am for love.

## *Love by Air mail*

I wait a whole day till the new morning
and when I hear the doorbell.
Like a dream, planes fly and boats sail
and I long for your love by air mail.

Remember the night with snow and hail.
Entwined together it was like a tale.
And how we crawled from pub to pub.
Running to shelter till we lost our breath
.

It's midnight now and morning is near.

I can not sleep yet, just waiting to hear.

Your voice and see your lips tremble.

On the pages of your letter by air mail.

How then there is no news of you.

Just a few words will put me at ease.

I wish if you could only see how I feel.

You didn't send your love by air mail.

## *Love is...? A Woman*

It took millions of years

for the Earth to evolve.

And for God to create Adam

at the top of the tree of evolution

and to make him complete

He created Eve out of Adam's ribs.

So the soul of love came into being

in the shape of a woman.

What about the beauty of a woman?

Is it really a matter of eyes or heart?

And what of the first love?

Is it not the need to produce?

Human as a demon or an angel

with love and hate in their hearts

and raging fire of jealousy

to save or kill as in peace or war.

Affairs of heart are the essence of life
and the aim of attraction is love.
The force of destruction is the hate
toiling with our future and fate.
But a precious gem lies just under
our ribs called a sweetheart.
Without which the notion of God
has no meaning at all.

Love is the essence of life.
Love is a man like Adam.
Love is a woman like Eve
a sweetheart from Adam's rib.

## *Troubled Soul*

Oh! My troubled soul.

Do I offer you that moment?

The moment of joy and passion.

Joy that pounds away concealed

into my blood stream.

The very essence of life and love

that impedes my way.

The random breath and heart beat

regrets I have no more to say.

But once and for all.

Oh! Tell me how to comfort you.

Make you feel serene.

Sudden surge in life that brings

waves of fear on the face of courage.

Is it the only way to be happy?

Strange thoughts always to follow.

Love that brings sorrow.

Oh! No. Let me say this

but once and for all.

Oh! My troubled soul.

## *Puffing Our Tomorrows*

Sharing sweets and gums was so much fun.

Daily stroll out on the beach in the sun.

I still hear your laughter echo in the air.

There was so much love for us to share.

Lots of promises we did make

carving our names on the trees.

I hear our names being called

by each falling of the leaves.

What happened to your burning love?

Ashes of my heart will always glow.

Never to break free from our dreams

even if lull was louder than screams.

Bits of sweets and half-chewed gums,

some torn pieces of scarf that you kept.

These are gems of my life to collect.

Puffing our tomorrows like a cigarette.

# The Torments of Love

The grey front door of my memory
leads me to roam, in the lane of crypt.
Back and forth, rocking the boat of love
and shock her being to become insane.
Look at the praise, hugs and kisses
and her cradle of love is there.
My regrets and her wishes
and the torments of love that we share.

She was true, like a summer's day.

I danced to the rhythms of her smile.

Now, places of love are in decay

and gift of love has turned sterile.

By the grey front door of hope

I stand like a pillar of fame.

And wish that she'd be back

to make my life complete.

## *Love is...? To Look at You*

Like the root that hides

the well being of the plants.

It is our need that guides

love with the world at large.

Does the need tie us to our beliefs?

Or makes us reach for the future.

But we believe in the present

to hide our failures of the past.

As a hurricane brings death to a tree
and a new shoot comes into being.
So the storm of stress can break a love
and a new quest for love takes its place.

Love is to look at you and say.
Just how much I love you.

# *Heart of Gold*

My heart is a heart of gold
not to be packaged and sold
and reach the shelf of need.
Where she can choose
and put in her box of jewel
and then forget to use.

For sale? My soul for her soul.
It is never to be.
Her pride will not bounce
till she makes an offer to me.

My good luck has returned
with warm desires
to soothe the pain of burn.
Then the summer will end.

Dreams not sweet and tender
and passion never turns cold.

I have no past to remember
and no future to be told.

## *Promises*

Your cheek rests on my arm.
I seal your lips with kisses.
Tonight your feel is warm
and I make a few promises.

Like the glow in your eyes
I spring up a new surprise.
Be mine tomorrow
or meet sadness and sorrow.

I want to know that you
missed me in time of need.
I only have eyes for you
and with me, life you'll lead.

# *Touch of Healing*

Suppressed anger that screams
in my midnight dreams.
It's wrong to surge ahead and excel
your love for me, so it seems.

Is there a stranger between us?
Your love isn't what I used to know.
And the vow that we made
to live by the rules that we laid.

Let there be the end of it all.
You have reached your ceiling.
And yet my wounded soul
longs for your touch of healing.

## *Love is...? Her Gaze*

Like the vents of eruption

giving rise to the hills.

She opens her life and collects

her senses of the past.

Like the sparks

made by the clashes of her gaze.

She lights candles of love

deep in her heart.

Like a block of ice she melts

under the heat of quest.

So restless to meet with

a man of the plane.

Willing to lose her being

to be one and the same.

The destiny itself tends

to lend her a helping hand.

What's the state of her will?

Burnt by her hate.

Head high she stands

with great courage and nerve.

Trying to calm her anger

in war with love.

At the feet of her will

lies love with all its power.

Love is to lament on

the fury of the past.

Love is to lend a hand

to bring hate to half-mast.

## *Mist and Haze*

Hear over the walls of mist and haze.

And let your cold feelings run ablaze.

While, sort my senses and think of you.

You know what really you should do?

Blow your kisses and hugs in the air.

Flaunt your sweet words if you dare.

Show your shock to shed like tear.

Flood your fear just to disappear.

And now spread your wings of patience.

There is no need to cheat, in essence.

So don't let your dreams catch cold.

Because love can't be bought or sold.

# *Young Crush*

Tender heart of a young crush of twelve.

At the brink of awakening sensual sense.

Aches, pains and feelings never felt before.

Pounds her veins profusely forever more.

Restless to see him then a long deep sigh!

A blush to her cheeks and her heart defy

the new heartbeats, she's grown to admire.

A new wave of youth she is to acquire.

A ghost of crush haunts her day and night.

She'll have to calm herself to face the fright.

To turn her tears into a burst of laughter

and happily live with it now and thereafter.

## *Once Again!*

Once again! I am without a friend.

Amidst uproar I found my silence.

Once again! In sadness and sorrows.

Solitude! I'm glad to have you around.

Once again! The blue summer sky

stares at me as the clouds pass by.

Once again! My hopes turned shy

and my broken heart thinks why?

Once again! I hear a sad cry.

The cry of the days gone by.

Once again! My love is lost

and now I just want to die.

## *Parts of Life*

Mood? A changing phase.

Romance? A sweet affair.

Love? An intriguing case.

Passion? A gust of hot air.

Mood, romance, love and passion

arranged like a show of fashion.

Youth? A stage of age.

Body? A burning desire.

Face? A cage to capture.

Beauty? A blaze to admire.

Youth, body, face and beauty

born and raised like a duty.

Love! A dream of heaven.

Life! A desire to live.

These parts of life ready to excel.

Made for us in heaven or hell.

## *Princess!*

Princess! Like a bud, of a bright yellow rose.

She smiles joy and a bunch of care for keeps.

Pure! A moonlit night face, acting her pose.

She is a dream child, a beauty as she sleeps.

She shows more than what she knows?

By a blink she stops the tide of the sea.

She wants all her wishes to come true.

At once, in a matter of a minute or two.

A child with a wish to fight against all
things special and the folks of fame.
She is nine and speaks about lost soul.
Hungry to know more that's her aim.

She questions life and its pros and cons.
Points her finger away from hectic norms.
Her belief shows like a smile in her eyes.
She is a dream child! A dazzle in disguise.

## *Love is...? The Captain of the Ship*

When the ship of love begins to sink
and heart takes no action to abandon.
What then if love seeks revenge
from the captain of the ship.

How to be sane without love that feeds life
with the reasons and reasoning to live.
It is easy to be what we are not meant to be
and very hard to be what we are.

If sanity is the price for the peace of mind
then let there be madness all around.
For it is madness that gives credence to love
whether we live or die in its search.

Love is the food of life.
Love is the sanctuary of soul.
Love is the ship of sanity.
Love is the inheritance for us all.

## *Longs for Love*

She longs for love when I close the door.

"Don't touch me," and she cries even more.

She sobs till I kiss her and then she's glad.

Wearing a smile on my lips makes her sad.

I would like to forget her but she is there.

Can't get her out, we've too much to share.

Some day she will repent when I'm gone.

Lost love is like the sunset after the dawn.

## *Memories*

Memories that live inside me
aren't so easy to leave behind.
Like the footsteps that you left
and echoes of, "do not try to find."

Do I play the tunes of your steps?
And feel the warmth of your sigh.
Dancing close two hearts one soul.
For love you didn't say goodbye.

The feelings that sweep my heart

can't wipe the mark of your steps.

And if you recall what you've said

when you left me alone tears to shed.

Still, here I stay with my only dream

that may come true in one morning.

I'll ask you when we meet someday.

Please come back to me. Come back.

## *Love is...? One Who Accepts*

It is in the name of one who accepts
love and hate or patience and anger.
It is the fate or the action that we take
to be safe in love or make life a danger.

If one likes to be with the guest
and one is not sure of what to expect.
Fate is the deed not done in earnest
and action may not yield right effect.

It is not easy to decline or disagree
with the gift of embrace and prelude.
If love turns into a river of tears
patience becomes a long-lasting feud.

Love is the one who accepts.
Love is to have patience.
Love is to wonder what if?
Love is to be patient and patient.

# I *Was Lucky*

You said I was lucky to have you
but I was in for a surprise.
I thought I couldn't fall in love.
Yet I have your face in my eyes.

It was a fall of a foolish heart.
Didn't know my life will fall apart
And my dreams with you were true.
A speck in my eyes that was you.

How to keep you secured in my net.

So hard you are trying to get free.

Leave me in midstream you mustn't.

I'm enslaved in your love can't you see?

I will wear a hush on my lips

and wait for you till the sunrise.

My love is strong and won't slip.

Sitting by the fire you will realise.

## *A Talking Clock*

Like a talking clock
she pours out her feelings
each minute of the day.
Like the chill of the season
she freezes in her thoughts
and there's no more to say.

Like a colorful butterfly
she has caught the eyes
of a man made of fire.
Same as the moving sands
her thoughts flow
from my needs to his desire.

Her lips try to reveal lies
and her gesture hides the truth.
Naked facts of our affair are
the lack of love in her feelings.
But I'll show that the only way
to true love is to reveal it all.
One day like the molten rocks
the wounds of her heart will erupt.

And her tears of regrets will flow
like a hot stream of lava.
So let's promise that from now on
no secrets will hide in our hearts.

## *Love is...? The Silent Words*

Her eyes whispered the silent words

into a soft corner of my heart.

And love echoed in all my veins

only to turn my joy into a sorrow.

Love means a gift of joy

instead I drown in grief.

Whereas she has sweet dreams

unaware of my pains.

Her silent words has shattered

the root of my patience.

And her love once so precious

has torn my heart into shreds.

Love is a daydream in the lonely nights.

Love is an escape from the real world.

Love is a pact of the feeble and the mighty.

Love is to speak in the silent words.

## *The Crossroad*

Torn ’tween love of the brown-eyed
and lust of the blonde.
I stand at the crossroad
of love and lust quite alone.

A girl I meet each morning
at ten past eight on the train.
She sits face to face
reading her Woman’s Own.
At times her eyes reach mine
and then rests as if to refrain.
She then sends me a smile
and lust darts from her eyes.

She mirrors the Monro's charms
blue eyes and long slender arms.
She speaks in melodious tone
and my heart starts to mourn

On my return at half past five
at times I sit near a plain looking girl.
She is tall and has lovely brown eyes.
With her soft voice her wishes flow
like the drifting sand in the sea of desert
and love simply slips her lips.
Flashes of her eyes
lure my love to a zooming height.

I so very much long to hold the blonde.

My soul cries for the love of the brunette.

Oh! Tell me not, for what am I

but rather than say what to do.

Shall I kill my hunger of lust?

Or play the eager tune of love?

Shall I try to change a man?

to be immune from both love and lust.

Torn 'tween the love of the brown-eyed

and lust of the blonde.

I stand at the crossroad

of love and lust quite alone.

## *Just You and Me*

Files on my desk

phone to my ear.

And I only see

you far and near.

One more day to go

before I see you again.

You are my love.

Your love is mine.

So let there be.

Just you and me.

## *Love is...? The Strength*

Like the strength of Samson
which lay hidden in his hair.
Body holds the secret of poise
expressed by the eyes of a man.
Kings and queens have fought to win
the war of love.
And in the field of emotion
have lost their craves to impulse.

Once lost in the depths of eyes
there is no way out except through
the door leading to the house of hurt.

If held under the shade of lure
love becomes like a brittle bone?
Even a little weight of doubt
breaks the bond and flings
trust like debris in space above.

Loss of charm isn't like losing
ourselves amidst people in need.
They are happy to live and die
with or without love.
So if they are removed from
living normal way of life.
Is it any wonder that they
refuse to abide by the rule.

Love is the strength of Samson.

Love is a desire to be just one.

Love is to be without fear of hurt.

Love is to be wilful like Delilah.

## *Endless Night*

In the dark and endless night
I turn to see if you really want me.
A play of dream is in your sight
but quite unaware of my being.

Am I just some one around you?
That you call in times of need.
Maybe a vent for your ego to burn
the urge and expel the fume.

Are we ends of the facing pole?

That we fight and do not agree.

You say my love has no soul.

Yet I have you. You must see.

One day you will see that I

need your love and care.

Life, alone is cruel to live.

So let's live our lives together.

## *The Queen of My Heart*

To be the best and win my heart
she stood alone against the norm.
Even before I laid my eyes on her
she faded like a candle in the storm.

Did I know her feelings and desires?
And demands of her sensual youth.
She was a diamond in the ring of my life
though she was a dying star in my heart.

Can't say if I have loved
women like her before.
Feel for her, I am fascinated
especially when I am not in love.

This is the secret she was to know
that I did wish her to be my wife.
But now that we've fallen apart
she isn't the queen of my heart.

## Love is...? Your Hypnotic Words

Like the opening words of the story

with your hypnotic words

you caught my heart.

But the ending was at the mercy

of your love

which ended even before the start.

Love at first sight was so brief

not long enough to take root.

A little dispute left a big enough

hurt never to heal.

My love is now upside down
this I can not bear.
And if you are happy with yours
then there is no reason to fear.

Love is to value the life of others.
Love is for all to see.
Love is to bear all the pains.
Love is just to be.

# *Christina!*

Christina! Oh Christina! What can I say?

You're so close to me yet so far away.

I have felt your heartbeats

like the beats of a distant drum.

Never stop love beats form your heart

I wish now, and for days to come.

Christina! Oh Christina! What can I say?

We are so close and  yet so far away.

## *Love is…? Mother of All!*

Mother of all power is a woman
of special breed.
Mother of all attraction is a woman
of distinct creed.
Mother of all passion is a woman
waiting her turns to charm.
Mother of all love is a woman
feeding her child in her arm.

A dark veil of mystique hides
her fame and fortune.
And she is always busy
to find a man of fine tune.

She is out of step but ahead

in the race like a winner.

How else can she hold?

Her place in high social scene.

She is the mother of all mystery

shrouded in the veil of virtue.

When challenged she can turn

into an enigma in haste.

Patience flows gently in her veins

often finds a way to refrain.

And kindness is what she'd like to wear

with hate of an ill-informed woman.

Love is the mother of all mystiques.

Love is the collection of all icons.

Love is the mother of all creation.

Love is the mother of a baby born

# *A Space Man*

Like a space man in his shuttle craft,

I'm lost in love and no link with you.

If you fly past then please contact.

The love locked loop is open to you.

I am trekking far in some other orbit.

Right on course but away from you.

Going round you just like the moon

pull me back in your heart's orbit too.

Like an astronaut I'm training to bear
the strain of love when it's not there.
And now that I'm in myself I can see.
I wasn't where I was supposed to be.

Travelling through the hazards of life
follow the track that leads to your heart.
You are there with all your loving care
and in your love I am being torn apart.

## *Remember You*

Slave I was in your love

but you had to set me free.

For I was a fool

and I did not know.

Love meant tears

and laughter too.

Now that I am alone

I long for you.

Still roaming by the shore.

In some special way.

Loving you even more

and trying to forget

many a time we met.

I will remember you.

# Melt Like Snow

My world of love stood still.
There was no hate in sight.
Then from the mouth of a man
a soft stream of polished words
fell upon the dark side of her praise.
Where I merged with hate
my conscience slowly died
and in her heart love melt like snow.

My pain of love wants to live.
But her lips are not wet with desire
and love never shouts from her eyes.

Her moves dance like a flame
and she has turned against
my heart, my love, my sweet love.
Ride a fabled horse in my dreams
and cease a full term of thrills in a day.
Catch a blaze of love in my anger
and sail or sink on the ship in danger.

My smile vanished in a dense mist
and love drowned in a sea of tears.
Love is a smile changing in laughter
and a sea of tears to sail thereafter.

## *Love is...? Duties of the Day*

Come sunshine or rain

we are bound to carry on

our duties of the day.

In doing so we sacrifice

most of our personal rights.

And as a human we are

supposed to live our lives

in the balanced way we want.

In the sunshine or rain
there is a war day and night.
Our duties have killed our rights.
Is it just to have sleepless nights?

But memory of our deeds
keep us awake till late
and our heart's desire torments us.
We did our duty but failed.

They say do your duties
your rights are enshrined.
Like yes and no
like love and hate.
They're two sides of the same fate.
Where there are no rights.
Let us proclaim now
that call of duty is too late.

Love is to lose yourself in duties.
Love is to fight for your rights.
Love is to fall in like a light feather.
Love is to bloom in all kinds of weather.

## *Dressed Not Veiled*

My choices are well defined

in line with the rules of the game.

When it comes to a business deal

I like to be sincere and straight.

My private affairs are to taste

and my love fully dressed not veiled.

Public acts are not for the people to see

and private affairs are for all to read.

It is not for the people to know

what goes on behind the closed doors?

Fully dressed lies leaked to be unveiled

and naked truth remains hidden inside.

Scale of justice shouts the lady is blind
and I know how helpless she is.
In case of the victims of the crime
I see the public and private affairs
speak aloud, together with the lies
and then hide, the truth beneath.

Hear the verdict. Now says the judge.
You are not guilty of telling lies
but found guilty of changing
the face of truth with the veil of lies.
The sentence is to love fully dressed
whole truth and lies without veil.

## *Moonshine*

In the gallery of my memory

hangs many images.

There's one face like moonshine

that will always scorch my soul.

She is the guest of my dreams.

Can't recall where we have met.

Am I for her and she for me?

We must be seeking the lost fate.

My love is the past memories.
See! All images have been fed
with my residual hatred and pride.
And all my memories have gone.

In betrayal of love and hate
I live for the day in clouds of dismay
longing to see that face in dreams
and joy would reign once again.

## *Parting*

Oh! Why did I meet her
where lone hearts were to meet?
Just to fall in love
to the point of betrayal.
Why then, I hear my heart
call her name?
Just before parting
till I see her again.

She prefers to stay in
and I like to roam around.
That's why we do not agree
to meet at a place and time.

I love her deeply

and she also longs to meet.

Why then, when we're face to face

our eyes are full with tears of grief?

I agree that my heart

may refuse to beat

against the longing heat

of a not so young flame.

And the loss of her love

may turn out to be the gain.

Forever not to be missed

and parting shall refrain.

A flash of smile in her eyes
lights the dark hours of my life.
Her gesture is the image of my trust
and her thoughts are my inner voice.
She is the reason that I live for
and my feelings live in her heart.
Her love will live and die with me.
Parting is not one of our parts.

## *Wine and Dine*

Tried pinball and the patience game.
Care for him. It's always the same.
His love is like a hazy sunshine.
To get through I've to wine and dine.

Try to play the games that lovers play.
It hurts me when he says no, not today.
When he wants me, I'm not so keen.
He really is a selfish mean machine.

My hungry love and thirsty desire
cry for more till the end of the call.
He is the only one I really admire.
For him I will die a hundred times.

## *Love is…? Like the Air*

What shape and colour is love?

Is it like the air I can not see?

Or the air that I breathe.

Yes! It is what lives inside me.

Without the breath of fresh air

I am sure to die.

But to be without love

life isn't going to say goodbye.

If love has left a big hole in my life.

Could I fill it with revenge?

Then who will be the winner?

Love? No. I would like to be the one.

Love is to run in the race of life.

Love is to say goodbye to strife.

## *Burnt Toast*

Leaning on the edge of perfection

I crawled out of my bed

and brewed a steaming cup of tea

to tickle the taste bud of my guest.

I asked if she'd like some toast with it.

She glanced at me and replied.

Yes, my hero! You are an angel.

Two lightly burnt toast if you could.

Does she like burnt foods?

Things like burnt toast?

Has she sensed my burning love?

Or is she making a fool of me.

This innocent guest of mine who lives in my heart.

Is she likely to play main role?

on the stage of my life.

As is the case in the affairs of heart.
We try to be nice even if it's not so
for the pleasure of the future half.
Often their demands stand to boast
and in the spirit of decency
you must not forget your host.

A cup of tea or a piece of burnt toast
may not fill her up or refresh her heart.
But as a guest she can stay in my life
with her wishes "till death us do part."
And I promise with all my intent
to fulfil the wishes of her heart.

## *Love is...? The Beauty*

She is more than the beauty of Venus.
Stops even the Sun when she smiles.
And her laughter radiates the waves of love
to reach my lonely heart full of desires.
There is nothing that is safe from her lure.
So I keep running to her just to make sure.

An army of admirers follows her around
like a sergeant in the parade of privates.
While she knows all the magical commands
of love to capture hearts of men in distress.
Who is to reveal that others may be untrue?
Their love is there only for a day or two.

She isn't what she seems to be
a real wild creature in the house of dolls.
Kind and loveable outside but hard
like a stone beneath the outer shell.
She is really the mine of diamond
hidden inside the crust of greed.

Love is to be away yet close to the heart.
Love is to forgive the betrayal of the past.
Love is to remember all things called love.
Love is to keep her safe and make it last.

## A Taste of Honey

Falling in love is like a taste of honey.

Once fallen you need a lot of money.

To buy her a diamond ring she'd admire.

And if you've no money love burns in fire.

## *Love is...? A Storm of Feelings*

A storm of feelings is raging

through the streets of my heart.

While waves of his escape

has swept away all my smiles.

I can see his whirling rage

pulling me in with all his lies.

What if he returns to take revenge?

To end all I have built over the years.

What will I do to save my sanity?

How will I cope from this fear?

Storm of feelings has left me in ruins.

The cycle of joy and pain to chase.

A hush now blows through my life.

And from me love has turned its face.

Love is a storm it begins with calm.

Love is like a storm it ends with rage.

## *Alien Being*

Make me suffer?

Must you?

Just say yes

to my needs of love.

There is nothing here

that you could do.

To make me love

some alien being.

## *Love is...? To Behold*

Called to behold God

at the peak of the mountain.

Blinded by the intense light

eyes couldn't see the face of gleam.

Was it not the wonder of faith?

A sermon to teach love.

Didn't he believe that he has seen?

Brighter than the brightest light.

He trusted the words of wisdom

spoken to him in time.

It is the unison that reveals

the face of the abstract being.

Believing the effects of miracles

and to see the countless face of love.

Came down with a vision of the world

trying to be at peace with itself.

There is a place to be in times of need

when love is there to look after and feed.

Love is divine

it's divine to be in love.

Love is to see the miracles of faith.

Love is to give whatever it takes.

## *Death by Misadventure*

Anger burst into a flame of hate
when she found me with other girls
and took her life with a drug overdose.
I was appalled and full of grief to know
the day news reported the verdict
of her death as “death by misadventure.”

She revealed the name of her love
in the note she had left behind.
I had seen her with other boys
and this thought did not occur
that she could have loved me.
Did she sow the seed of jealousy?
and all this backfired on her.

She really played a dangerous game
to win my love she lost her life.
Instead of winning love at all cost
she won no response at all.
When she tried to make me jealous
she gave me no cause for concern.

Love is my strength
and my weakness too.
But I have learnt a lesson
from her tragic death.
Never to hide my feelings
in the affairs of heart.

## *Love is…? The Snowflakes*

From the heap of the snowflakes
a snowman came to be.
Pointing her finger at me
"I was like that heap!" shouted she.
Cold and calm showed no remorse
for what I ask her do.
Didn't want to know how she felt
and imposed my will in need.

In her view I was the reason
for her nervous break down.
And why she tried to take
her life so many times.
So why did I save her?

From the tragic death.

If I didn't love

in peace I should have her left.

Was I like that heap of snowflakes?

Warm feelings do flow in my veins.

She was just naive about love

and how I showed it to be.

My feelings were so deep

and acts so cool and calm.

She did not believe me

For her I had deep love in my heart.

Love is the flake of immense magnitude.

Love is beyond doubt in every one's reach.

## *Touch Me Not*

Beauties on show, is an invitation to treat.

Lovely like flowers! Cool white or red hot.

I like to admire them and get a little closer.

They are right to say look but touch me not.

I argue about pros and cons of the show.

Is it not to please me? I may shout aloud?

My needs are above the needs of others

and my deeds above their personal goals.

Beauty is an inducement to breed

and is likely to accede to my needs.

And at times her wishes come alive

by the magical touch of her choice.

Success of shun gives her the strength

to play Goddess of the hour in need.

Would she agree to my next advance?

How I wish I knew. Oh! How I wish.

## *Beguiling Eyes*

I only have to look at her face

to tell a happy or a sad tale.

But to read what's in her heart

I gaze into her beguiling eyes.

Masked with the layers of lashes

hard to bear the demise of vision.

Begins to make up for the loss of

stolen scenes of her dreamy eyes.

Beguiling eyes! Cast a shadow of charm
upon my heart not yet aroused by grief
and draw me towards her to reveal it all.
Just by one look, a deep beguiling look.

My heart, beats to capture her vision of love
and I sing the way she makes every move.
Her love's with me every moment of the day
very safe under her watchful beguiling eyes.

## *Love is...? The Edge of Lunacy*

Like the downpour of the rain
her memories keeps streaming
in the depths of my heart.
When urge reaches the edge of lunacy
the bank of patience burst to flood
the domain of love.
But deep in the lakes of life
I have buried her hate.
What incites the face of innocence?
To change and turn into a fire of fury.
Is it the spark created by the wish?
Of anger or heat of passion.
Am I the winner or the loser?
Or may be a victim or a victor.
Is it my ego talking over the heads
Of envy for the state I am in?.

To live in the dry lake of sentiments
without being hounded by a soul mate.
Driven by the fear of frosty encounters
with a single aim to live life with love
and what of people starved of love?
For whom love is an alien being
with no partners and hungry needs,
they aim their lives to live alone.

Love is like the rain falling at the verge of life.
Love is to fill the emptiness of the deep desire.
Love is to bury all the wrong doings of the past.
Love is to incite the spark of innocence to last.

# *The Face*

The face of love in my heart

is not the same that I see.

Though the gestures are alike

but not the face I call love.

Just because I take care of you

does not mean that I am in love.

So tell me why do I feel so hurt

when you don't see when I am there.

What if I am not in love with you?

I do want to know

that you do need me

more and more to fall in love.

You and I! Could we live together?

Without the burden of pretence

\That I love you or you love me.

Just know that we live with each other.

# *Love is...? The Green Meadows*

Vast spans of the green meadows;

it's so pleasing and blessed.

But inside its green blanket

lie wonders of the world

which only the revolt in its heart

can reveal skeleton of war,

and flesh of peace

along with the shroud of love.

Hands of the future

hold pasture of the past

to spawn the secret

of the meadows to last.

Powers of the past
laid claims to its beauty
and rulers of the future
have fixed their gaze.

How to save chaste
from coercion of their trust?
When servers proclaim
to be the masters of faith.

They have lost their honesty
and all of their kindness.
Do the hands
of death scorch them?

Was it the other face
of love thy neighbor?
So that the valued meadows
bids to ask for a favour.

They shut their eyes
but aim is in view.
Though trapped in despair
they still wait in queue.
And from the dark
edges rise a glow
and a spark of distrust
flares from the rooted faith.

They have lost their intrigue
and help of public at large.
They have no cast or creed
and no moral moorings or barge.

Nature's laws no longer
rule their lives.
And an emotion
like love has turned sterile.

Love is to walk on the meadows hand in hand.
Love is the ruler of our hearts and minds.
Love is the seed and the fruit of the future.
Love is what we all strive to nurture.

## Hostage for Life

He held me hostage for life by one look
and now? Now his home is in my heart.

He chants words like honey and my love
and I see no way to escape from his hold

He flirts with other girls without a care.
How could I forgive him it is not fair?

Yes! My search for a solution goes on
while I sink deeper and deeper in his love.

## *Accusing Silence*

Silence is the poetry of peace
though I've much to scream.
Could I be without his strife?
For years he's been my star.
The only reason, is loss of trust
in him for my accusing silence.

His lips open the gate of words
to wound my heart with grief.
And stares of his jealous eyes
plants the seed of hate to grow.
She gets his love and praise
could I bear this even if I try?

It's no use, even if I shout like mad.
To defend he will just say how sad.
He will offer wine to shower peace
and spread his charm like cheese.
He wins me over to his wicked ways
with no remorse at all to what he says.

Like any one I will burst in anger
one day, at a time of my choosing.
And I will lay him aside just to drop
from the peak of love to the pit of hate.
Then no glass of wine will talk peace
and I'll have my long due revenge.

# Love is...? The Roaming Clouds

Drifters in love

like the roaming clouds.

Do not know

when they'll meet.

They have to endure

hurt given by their own

to live and face

the world on their own feet.

Like Nimbus and Cumulous

they might rain at any plane.

Like young and old

they all discover.

Love knows no bounds.

No limit of age
no cast or creed.
Just love's their need.

Can't scoop a drop
from the Ocean.
So the drifters in love
settle for eternal thirst.
It's not enough
but they could survive
without the feeling
called love in their hearts.

Love is a sentiment drifting like clouds.
Love is a weak heart longing to survive.

## *First Look*

Like the first gulp of the fresh air

she filled my life with longing.

Like the first face of the "C" moon

she took my heart, at first look.

Seemingly confused and bemused

with a feeling of strange magnitude,

overwhelming effect upon my heart

made me restless for days and weeks.

My heart shall only cease to bleed

when her false pride begins to melt

and the first look shall rule my life

till she returns her love with mine.

Must find a way to make her realize.

She needs my love to adorn her life.

Without her first look and first love

I won't want to live even for a day.

## *I Know*

I know you're not mine.

At least drink this wine.

Let's refresh our minds.

We are two of a kind.

Now let's get to talk.

Not mimic or mock.

Let us start afresh

to end this mess.

## *Love is...? Hidden in Our Hearts*

Face isn't the mirror that shows.

What is in our minds?

But we can see looking into eyes

the feelings hidden in our hearts.

We learn to betray the trust

and minds weave a web of lies.

Lips do reveal our thoughts

and truth always hides in our hearts.

Love has happiness of countless shades
shown by gestures or fired from lips.
But neither gestures nor words can cause
the wounds, by mere look of our eyes.

Love is discovery of a new heart.
Love is a pain and pleasure at war.
Love is a spark lit by a need to admire.
Love is a dress with no shape or size.

## *Like a Candle*

Hate for love! Is the reward for me?
For I lost my life in your thoughts.
Wish heat of my belief burn your soul
and you melt like a candle in my love.

In the deepest corner of my heart
glows many faces of your hate.
Just tell me how shall I equate
your actions with my fate.

When feelings change for real

and your hate turns into love.

That's when you will see

the changing face of my love.

Your conceit you may use

to drown my pride.

Or be quiet as a hush

and change your hate for love.

## *Love is...? A Change of Heart*

The craving of our wild needs

holds all sins of the creatures of faith.

A superior being destined to seek

the arms of a young flame.

They do not know

if the heat of passion will keep

blaze of longing alive

or love will have a change of heart.

They play all cards of emotion

even force of fear to please.

If it isn't the arms of charm

they make good use of love.

To bear fruits of efforts

and call them their own.

They know about their prize

to be the wave of change.

Others are not so happy
to hurt their own kind.
They're content with the change
and leave the rest for others to find.
Being the winner is not enough
they are bound for what they do.
Their unfair deeds are to hate others
for, then love dies a painful death.

Love is to have a change of heart.
Love is a force that attracts at first sight.
Love is the patience when we feel sad.
Love is to hold lover's arm like mad.

## *Love is...? The Force of Life*

Countless avenues to explore

and millions of ways to show.

The bonding of the force of life

reveals the secret of the cosmos.

Vision may hinder our thoughts

love may not be what it may seem.

And all our efforts depend upon

the strength of our sensuous zeal.

But the cosmic force may draw
the ends to collide in such a way
so as to destroy the very creation
with spin of love over the years.

Love is the force of life.
Love is the bonding of souls.
Love is a wish to live forever.
Love is to explore and explore.

## *Dating*

They told me dating for a year or two
will make love grow between me and you.
So the sound of bell keeps emanating
and year after year we still go on dating.

What can I say when you really know?
How long courtship is supposed to go?
I love you and that's why it's so irritating
and year after year we still go on dating.

Now time has come and I must decide.
To have you around me on your terms.
And to keep the promises that you made
a few years ago when we began to date.

Tell me how to make you realize.
I need love all the time all the while.
So I am waiting for you to marry me
or please set me free from dating.

## *Love is...? Other Beings*

Other beings in the universe!

Could they have the same passion?

Affairs of heart and deep feelings

smiles and laughter, tears and pain.

Or the instinct called procreation

which bears the feeling called love.

Other beings! Do they feel hate?

And budding love withers away

even before it has the time to seed

in hearts and minds of all in need.

Sometimes love is used and abused

in each and every cast and creed.

Love is not the only tool to use
people find ways and means to rule
hearts and minds of other beings.
They say, " I hate you" to inject a toxin
and send their subjects into fury.
Giving a sense of distrust all around.

Love is a mission that rules the creation.
Love is a weapon of mass seduction.
Love is a toxin that calms our desire.
Love is an urge that sets our hearts on fire.

## *Next to Her Skin*

I was like the armour, next to her skin
to hide her from the eyes of the dentist.
When asked, about her affair with him
like a bare-faced liar, she denied it all.
And about her fling with the taxi driver?
"Moustache!" she said. "I liked about him."

Today I can see. What future holds for me?
Through a plate-glass window of intrigue.
And under the umbrella of the blue sky
stands a sour taste, unlike the banana split.
Her smile from the corner of her eyes
hints an affair with a man surely she'll deny.

## *Love is...? Temptation*

Temptation is a sign of mental crave
or a war on wants in need.
And lure of love is a heart to know
for a man or a woman indeed.

Basis of love is unlike a business
here need is man, money and material.
But to love you need hearts and minds
and a great deal of care and attention.

Life fulfilled is like a frame caught in time

it only shows the end of the last event.

Though tempting it is to wait for someone

to entice and indulge in an affair.

Love is a temptation.

Love is to entice a soul.

Love is to cry in anger.

Love is to forgive and forget it all.

## *Brown Sugar!*

Brown sugar!

Where is your charm?

And your laughter

that aroused my soul.

And your love!

That has taken it all.

Brown sugar!

Once I saw myself

in your eyes.

And I was to live

in your heart.

Was I a fool or a wise?

It wasn't right

from the very start.

Do you see?

What I have become?

Your love is dying

like the summer mist.

Without your love

I am lonely.

Like a shooting star

destined, not to exist.

## Words Like This

People say this in so many ways
I say this in my words like this.

## *Love is...? All of These and More*

Love is a face we see when we close our eyes.

Love is a faith seen in the mirror of trust.

Love is the spawn of tears and laughter.

Love is the fusion of emotional needs.

Love is to meet with a lonely heart.

Love is to reach out to a special friend.

Love is to live with diverse views.

Love is the peace in times of war.

Love is to calm a restless soul.

Love is to search for a treasure of trust.

Love is a hate to live alone.

Love is to find a path of patience.

Love is to burn strife in the fire of zeal.

Love is to control passion and rage.

Love is the peaks and troughs of feelings.

Love is a spell that torments our hearts.

Love is to wait without tears.

Love is to be kind with the feelings of hate.

Love is to sense the affairs of heart.

Love is to know each other's feelings.

Love is to perform and please.

Love is a breath of fresh air.

Love is allure and uplifting of soul.

Love is simply to give it all.

## Questions Have Been Asked

*Questions have been asked about love*
*and more often than not have been answered*
*with love.*